W9-BKB-903

ADOPT ME!
JOIN THE
PET SET

KINGFISHER
LONDON & NEW YORK

X

Copyright © Macmillan Publishers International Ltd 2023
Published in the United States by Kingfisher
120 Broadway, New York, NY 10271
Kingfisher is a division of Macmillan Children's Books, London
All rights reserved

ISBN: 978-0-7534-7951-3

Distributed in the U.S. and Canada by Macmillan,
120 Broadway, New York, NY 10271

EU representative: Macmillan Publishers Ireland Ltd, 1st Floor, The Liffey Trust Centre, 117-126 Sheriff Street Upper, Dublin 1, D01 YC43.

All information is correct as of December 2022.

Library of Congress Cataloging-in-Publication data has been applied for.

Written by Eddie Robson
Designed, edited and project managed by Dynamo Limited

Kingfisher books are available for special promotions and premiums. For details contact: Special Markets Department, Macmillan, 120 Broadway, New York, NY 10271.
For more information, please visit
www.kingfisherbooks.com.

Printed in China
9 8 7 6 5 4 3 2 1
1TR/0423/WKT/RV/128MA

MIX
Paper | Supporting
responsible forestry
FSC® C116313

ADOPT ME!
JOIN THE PET SET

KINGFISHER
LONDON & NEW YORK

CONTENTS

WELCOME TO
ADOPTION ISLAND

Adopt Me! is one of Roblox's most popular MMORPGs, with over 30 billion visits since it went live in 2017.

Originally, *Adopt Me!* was about parents and babies. Players chose to be one or the other, and a parent would **adopt a baby** and set up a home for them. However, in 2019 the option of **adopting pets** was introduced, and the popularity of the game skyrocketed.

Players can still choose to play as babies. But the focus of the game is far more on the **pets**, which can be collected and traded with other players.

IN YOUR NEIGHBORHOOD

MAKE YOURSELF AT HOME!

The map is divided into two main areas. The Neighborhood is where the players' homes are located, while the main shops and facilities are on Adoption Island.

Your home in *Adopt Me!* is where you'll spawn into the game. Keep in mind that each time you visit the game, you'll be in a new server with different players, so your home will be in a different place in the Neighborhood.

Welcome to the Neighborhood!

With the Premium Plots gamepass, which costs 449 Robux, you can put your house on Adoption Island instead of in the Neighborhood, enabling you to travel around faster and earn more Bucks.

CREATURE COMFORTS

You can redecorate your home, furnish it, and even change it for another house entirely. When you want to do that, you can sell the old house for a lower price than you paid. The price includes all furniture in the house—you can't move furniture from one house to another.

Buying a **water cooler**, **coffee maker**, or **tea set** for your home will enable you to fulfill thirst needs without going anywhere or spending more money.

Decorate your house however you want.

The Money Tree costs 1,450 Bucks, but it'll pay for itself. Before long you can collect up to 100 Bucks a day from its branches.

TINY HOME

Price: Free / 240 Bucks

When you start a new game, you'll spawn in a single-story **Tiny Home**, which has three rooms and basic furniture. You can't throw parties here—it's not big enough!

FAMILY HOME

Price: 489 Bucks / 99 Robux

This has a similar design to the **Tiny Home**, but it has five rooms spread across two floors. You can buy it as part of the **Starter Pack** for 99 Robux. It's still not big enough for a party though!

PIZZA PLACE

Price: 500 Bucks

You can make your home in a shop, if you want. The cheapest option among them is the **Pizza Place**, which has an advantage over the cheaper houses in that you can host parties in it!

TREEHOUSE

Price: 800 Bucks

This has the same number of rooms as the **Tiny Home**, so in that sense it's not much of an upgrade. But c'mon, it's in a tree! How cool is that?

ESTATE

Price: 972 Bucks

The next step up from the **Family Home** is the **Estate**, and it has six rooms. It looks like it has a third story on the left, but actually it just has two.

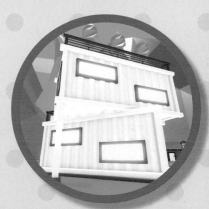

There are many, many more houses you can buy—all the way up to the **Luxury Apartments**, which cost 8,000 Bucks! Better get saving . . .

TOUR OF THE TOWN

EVERYTHING YOU NEED IS HERE!

Stepping through the gateway in the Neighborhood will take you to Adoption Island. Let's take you around some of the shops and facilities you'll find there.

NURSERY

The **Nursery** is located at the center. This is where **babies** are adopted, and the Age-o-Matic in the Adoption Center enables players to switch between **baby** and **adult**. But it's also the place to buy **eggs**. Doug, Holly, and Sir Woofington can be approached to purchase the game's three main **permanent eggs**. The current **limited egg** can be bought from the gumball machine. With a **VIP gamepass**, you can access the VIP room where free food and drinks are available and the **Retired Egg** is sold.

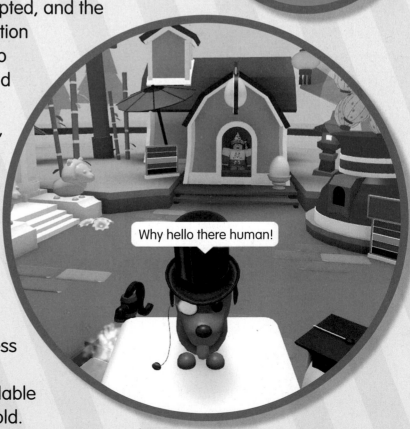

Why hello there human!

PLAYGROUND

Pets and babies can be brought here to play when they get bored. It includes a special **pet park**.

The main in-game currency of *Adopt Me!* is Bucks, which you can earn by doing things like taking your pet to the playground or the hospital.

HOSPITAL

You'll need to come here if a pet or baby is sick. You can cure sickness by feeding the Healing Apple to the sick pet or baby. Alternatively, you can sit on the bed in the operation room or speak to Doctor Heart.

CAMPSITE

Whether you like it or not, babies and pets LOVE camping and will want to go every three in-game days. This means a trip to the **Campsite**, which is way over on the other side of Adoption Island, making it the most annoying location to travel to! However, there are other needs you can fulfill there. There are s'mores that cost 5 Bucks, free marshmallows if your pet is hungry, and sleeping bags if they're sleepy. You can also rent a **cabin**, but that costs 200 Bucks! And immediately after fulfilling your pet's need to go camping, you can use the showers.

Relax with some s'mores!

TOY SHOP

Run by Javier, this shop sells toys and small vehicles like pogo sticks and roller skates.

VEHICLE DEALERSHIP

This place sells larger vehicles like bikes, cars, helicopters, and planes, and is run by Rich.

ACCESSORY SHOP

This is the one that's shaped like a ship. Pet accessories are sold here, and you can also open chests for random items.

For when your cat needs a hat.

SCHOOL

Sometimes your pet will feel the need to learn something, so you'll have to take them to the **School**, which is run by a teacher called Emma. Just being in the School will fulfill this need, and your pet can also eat, drink, and sleep there. Shane will teach your pet **tricks**. Babies can use the beds and can also take the teacher's apple for food.

PIZZA SHOP

This important location is shaped like a slice of pizza. You can get pizza and drinks here when a pet or baby is hungry or thirsty. You can also fulfill the **Pizza Party** need, which is a completely different thing from hunger. If you take a job here, you can earn 10 Bucks per pizza as a **Chef**, or 15 Bucks per minute as a **Waiter**, **Waitress**, or **Manager**. Your pet's needs will pause while you work, but you can use the job to get free food—taking a pizza with you after the **Pizza Shop** closes for the day is a good idea.

Grab a slice

Now Hiring!

NOW HIRING! COOKS, SERVERS & MANAGERS

NOW HIRING! COOKS, SERVERS & MANAGERS

Pets love pizza parties.

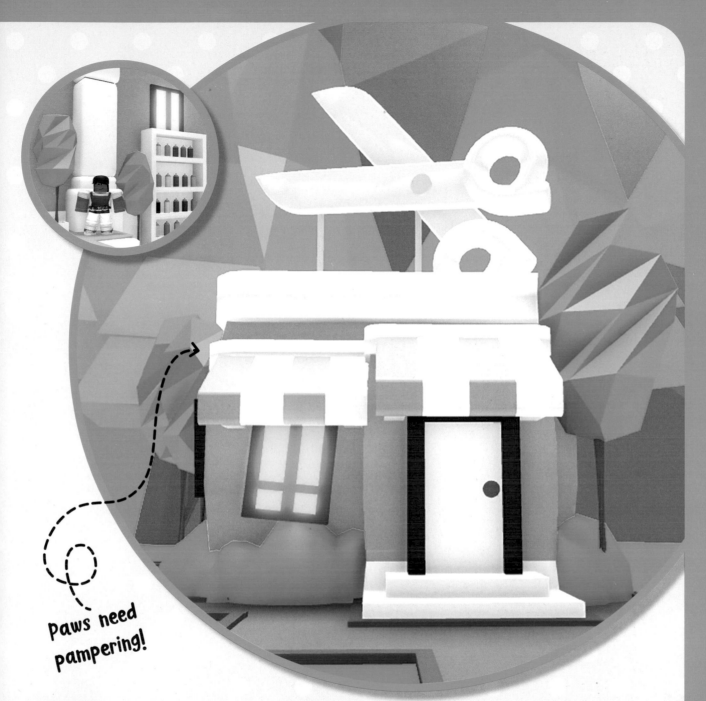

Paws need pampering!

SALON

Sometimes pets will want pampering and beauty **treatments** at the **Salon** run by Ella. This is another location where players can take a job (paying 15 Bucks per minute) and use tools like the scissors or hair dryer.

Better still, the colored hair sprays can temporarily change the color of your pet . . . if you've ever wanted a green dog! The waiting area has free donuts, and employees can also access a staff area containing food and drink for pets.

COFFEE SHOP

This is one of the first buildings you will see after entering Adoption Island from the Neighborhood. It's run by Archer and Beetrice, who is a bee and very vocal about workers' rights. You can buy tea, coffee, and cookies here—and also **Honey**, which does cost Robux and is used to tame and acquire bees.

ICE CREAM SHOP

This is next to the **Pizza Shop** and is run by Elsa. Penguins skate around the ice inside. You can buy ice cream here for a Buck, or buy a Golden Goldfish with Robux in order to obtain a King Penguin. You can have up to three scoops on your ice cream . . . see what happens if you try to add a fourth!

FARM SHOP

The **Farm Shop** is run by Justin and Lily, and features a range of food and drink for sale. You can also buy Golden Lavender with Robux to attract Ladybugs and add one to your pet inventory.

PET SHOP

This is at the center of the island. You can buy toys and food for your pets here, most of which can be bought for Bucks. However it also sells a range of pets which can only be bought with Robux.

Is your dream pet inside?

SKY CASTLE

This floats above the island and can be reached by paying 5 Bucks for a hot air balloon ride or riding a pet that can fly. The shop here sells potions as well as the **Cobra**, which costs 500 Robux.

TOOLS OF THE TRADE

SWAPPING CAN BE SWEET!

Exchanging pets with other players is a big part of *Adopt Me!*, and it's the only way to get a hold of pets that were part of limited events. You can offer multiple items in one trade, so you can trade several low-value ones for a high-value one.

FAIR GAME

It can be hard to judge what makes a **fair trade**. Different things have different values to different people. If there's a particular pet you want to complete a set, and they don't come up for trade very often, you might be willing to let a more valuable one go. But the game will flash up a **warning** if a trade seems unfair—and scam trades can be reported. Don't let anyone pressure you into making a trade—you can't be reported for declining. You can always walk away!

Be careful when trading— Never trade items for Bucks or Robux! Only use the trade menu to trade items, or you may get scammed. Stay safe!

Okay

NEVER TRADE ON TRUST

You'll sometimes see people offering **"trust trades,"** where you give them a pet for free, and they promise to do another trade where they give you a pet for free. DO NOT AGREE TO THIS. It almost always means the other person will just walk off with your pet! There's no reason to do it that way. Trades should be trades.

Study your inventory . . .

Players tend to be attracted to the pet they can see, so if you want to trade a pet, equip it. Otherwise, a lot of players will ignore what you want to trade and offer for the equipped one.

EGGSPLANATIONS

IT'S EGGS-CITING STUFF!

Of course, in the real world only certain types of animals hatch from eggs. But in *Adopt Me!* all kinds of animals hatch from eggs. To make an egg hatch, you need to carry out tasks or spend Robux on the Hatch Now! gamepass to skip this step.

As you play the game and earn money, you'll be able to buy more eggs. There's always a random element to which pet you get from an egg, but the more expensive the egg, the more likely it is you'll get a higher-rarity pet.

Some eggs are permanently available in the game, but there are also **limited event eggs**. These hatch pets that you can't get from other eggs, and the pets are usually themed (for instance, all the pets hatched from the **Ocean Egg** were sealife).

Here you see the Japan Egg. Hatching it can get you a Dugong, Tanuki, Ibis, Koi Carp, Leopard Cat, Red Crowned Crane, Spider Crab, Trapdoor Snail, Baku, or even a Maneki-Neko!

This tells you the probability of your egg hatching a sought-after legendary pet.

STARTER EGG

X

Cost: Free
Availability: Permanent
Chances:

Common	100%
Uncommon	0%
Rare	0%
Ultra-Rare	0%
Legendary	0%

It all starts here . . .

If you're new to the game, you'll get this **Starter Egg** for free from Sir Woofington. It's a **permanent egg** because it's never removed from the game, but you only ever get it once. You can't trade it either, which means you can't get it from another player. This is the egg with the most predictable outcome, since it will either hatch into a **Cat** or a **Dog**—so you can't get any pet above Common rarity from this egg.

CRACKED EGG

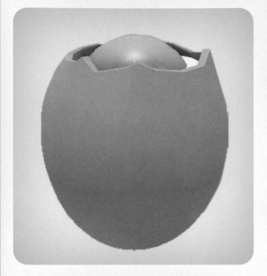

Cost: 350 Bucks
Availability: Permanent
Chances:

Common	45%
Uncommon	33%
Rare	14.5%
Ultra-Rare	6%
Legendary	1.5%

Due to being damaged, the **Cracked Egg** is the cheapest egg in the game—in fact, if you don't want to pay 350 Bucks for one, you can get one for free via Daily Rewards. Just log in for 30 days in a row. As you can see, the **Cracked Egg** has a very high chance of hatching a Common pet, so if you collect a lot of these, you'll end up with tons of Common pets. It hatches after four tasks are performed.

First trip to the salon

Unhatched

Nap time!

PET EGG

Cost: 600 Bucks

Availability: Permanent

Chances:

Common	20%
Uncommon	35%
Rare	27%
Ultra-Rare	15%
Legendary	3%

The **Pet Egg** is a normal, featureless egg. It's superior to the **Cracked Egg** since the chances of hatching a pet in the top three rarity categories is doubled. However, the most likely outcome is an Uncommon pet. All the pets that aren't limited or restricted to VIP passholders can be hatched from this egg. The **Pet Egg** must be bought from Holly in the Nursery or obtained by trading with other players. You need to perform five tasks to hatch it.

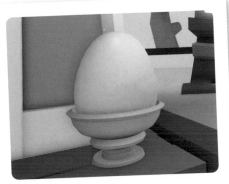

An egg-cellent purchase

Unhatched

Taking a stroll

ROYAL EGG

Cost: 1,450 Bucks
Availability: Permanent
Chances:

Common	0%
Uncommon	25%
Rare	37%
Ultra-Rare	30%
Legendary	8%

The **Royal Egg**, identifiable by its li'l crown, is by far the most expensive **permanent egg**—more than twice the cost of any other egg. But look at those stats—it has a 75% chance of hatching into a pet in the top three rarity categories and is guaranteed not to hatch into a Common pet. In particular, your chances of getting an Ultra-Rare pet are much better with this egg than any other. Sir Woofington sells this egg in the Nursery, and you'll need to do six tasks to hatch it.

Royal display egg

Out and about

RETIRED EGG

Cost: 600 Bucks
Availability: Permanent
Chances:

Common	20%
Uncommon	35%
Rare	27%
Ultra-Rare	15%
Legendary	3%

This egg was introduced in July 2022 when the 16 pets that had previously featured in **Cracked**, **Pet**, and **Royal Eggs** were moved to the **Retired Egg**.

The **Retired Egg** is available from the VIP room in the Nursery, which can only be accessed by purchasing a VIP pass for 750 Robux.

If you're not a VIP, you'll have to seek it out through trading. The types of pet available from this egg are: **Buffalo**, **Cat**, **Dog**, **Otter**, **Chocolate Labrador**, **Fennec Fox**, **Puma**, **Snow Cat**, **Beaver**, **Bunny**, **Rabbit**, **Snow Puma**, **Red Panda**, **Shiba Inu**, **Dragon**, and **Unicorn**. The cost and chances of obtaining a pet of each rarity are the same as the **Pet Egg**.

A free-range egg!

PET CATALOG

Adopt Me! has introduced a huge range of pets, and more are coming into the game all the time. The following pages take you through the main ones you're likely to encounter—and some of the more unusual ones too.

There are lots of variant versions of pets, but every pet can be obtained in **Neon** and **Mega Neon** form. Simply raise four pets of the same type until they're full-grown, then go to the **Neon Cave** underneath the bridge that leads from the Neighborhood to Adoption Island.

There you can place your four pets on each of the outer circles and fuse them into a Neon Pet. Each Neon Pet has areas of its body that glow a particular color. Mega Neon Pets, where the glowing areas cycle through all the different colors, can be made by fusing four Neon Pets of the same type.

Not all pets are animals . . . like this robot!

Some pets are special guests and are only available for a short time.

ALICORN

Rarity: Legendary
Availability: Permanent
Obtain With: Pet Egg,
Cracked Egg, Royal Egg

OK, you've almost certainly heard of **unicorns**. But **Alicorns**? This is another mythical beast—a cross between a **unicorn** and a **pegasus**. So, a unicorn that flies. You're most likely to hatch one from a **Royal Egg**.

The best of two magical worlds

ANCIENT DRAGON

Rarity: Legendary
Availability: Permanent
Obtain With: Pet Egg,
Cracked Egg, Royal Egg

There have been several reskins of the standard **Dragon**, but the **Ancient Dragon** (which has taken its place in the game's three main eggs) is a whole different design, with a Chinese-dragon-inspired look including curved horns and a beard.

Check out this ancient legend!

ANT

Rarity: Common
Availability: Permanent
Obtain With: Pet Egg, Cracked Egg

The **red Ant** in the game differs from a **real ant** in two important ways. It's bigger and it's also cuter, with beady black eyes. Hatch a few **Cracked Eggs** and you'll probably obtain one of these pretty quickly—22.5% of **Cracked Eggs** hatch an **Ant**.

> This pet is perman-ant!

AUSTRALIAN KELPIE

Rarity: Rare
Availability: Limited
Obtain With: Aussie Egg

Not to be confused with the shape-shifting **kelpies** of Scottish folklore, the **Australian Kelpie** is a breed of **sheepdog** that can come in a wide variety of colors. The one in the game has a black-and-tan coloring. There was a 13.5% chance of hatching one from an **Aussie Egg**.

> They come from a land down-under.

AXOLOTL

Rarity: Legendary
Availability: Permanent
Obtain With: 600 Robux

. . . .

The **Axolotl** is a critically endangered amphibian native to Mexico, whose natural lake habitats have been destroyed by urbanisation and pollution. They're usually brown in the wild, but the ones bred as pets are frequently pink. In *Adopt Me!* they can be purchased from the Pet Shop for 600 Robux.

Think pink.

BAKU

Rarity: Legendary
Availability: Limited
Obtain With: Japan Egg

The **Baku** is a creature from Japanese mythology, said to be made from the parts left over when the gods had created all the other animals. It also eats nightmares, which makes it a nice pet to have. It can only be hatched from the **Japan Egg**.

Dream a little dream of Baku

BANDICOOT

Rarity: Common
Availability: Limited
Obtain With: Aussie Egg

Made famous in the video-gaming world by the game *Crash Bandicoot*, the **Bandicoot** is a marsupial native to Australia and New Guinea. It had a 30% chance of hatching from the **Aussie Egg**, so may be fairly easy to find through trading.

There's no crashing this Bandicoot!

BEAVER

Rarity: Rare
Availability: Permanent
Obtain With: Pet Egg, Cracked Egg, Royal Egg

The **Beaver** is a large, industrious rodent that's more at home in the water than on land. It used to be available from the three main eggs but can now only be hatched from the **Retired Egg**, with a chance of just under 7%.

This pet goes with the flow.

BEE

Rarity: Ultra-rare
Availability: Permanent
Obtain With: Honey

. . . .

Bees are unusual—to adopt one you must go to the Coffee Shop and buy **Honey**, which costs 199 Robux (you can't buy it with in-game currency). This can be thrown in the Coffee Shop to tame a **Bee**. You have an 87.5% chance of getting a **Bee**, a 10% chance of a **King Bee**, and a 2.5% chance of a **Queen Bee**.

Sweet!

BUFFALO

Rarity: Common
Availability: Permanent
Obtain With: Retired Egg

. . . .

The **Buffalo** was one of the first Common pets to be introduced into *Adopt Me!* and one of the oldest pets to still be available in the game—though now only through the **Retired Egg**. A Halloween variant of this pet, the **Zombie Buffalo**, is mega-rare.

Roam with the Buffalo.

BULLFROG

Rarity: Common
Availability: Limited
Obtain With: Woodland Egg

The **Bullfrog** is actually a collective name for a whole group of large, aggressive frogs that live in various parts of the world. But the one in the game resembles an **American Bullfrog**. This was the Common pet hatched from the **Woodland Egg**.

Don't worry, be hoppy!

❌

CAMEL

Rarity: Uncommon
Availability: Permanent
Obtain With: Pet Egg,
Cracked Egg, Royal Egg

The **Camel** resembles a cross between the different breeds of **camel** that exist in the real world. It has two humps like a **Bactrian camel**, but its smoothness is more like a **dromedary**. A **Pet Egg** is your best chance of obtaining one.

One hump or two?

❌

CAT

Rarity: Common
Availability: Permanent
Obtain With: Starter Egg, Retired Egg

The **Cat** is the easiest pet to acquire in the game if you hatch it from the **Starter Egg** you get at the beginning. You only ever get one **Starter Egg** in a game, so if you hatch the **Dog**, the only way of getting a **Cat** is to trade for one or acquire a **Retired Egg**.

A purrr-fect pet

CERBERUS

Rarity: Legendary
Availability: Permanent
Obtain With: 500 Robux

This **three-headed dog** comes from Greek mythology, where it guarded the gate to the Underworld. It was introduced to *Adopt Me!* for the Halloween 2020 event but unusually became a permanent pet. It was moved to the Pet Shop where it can be bought for 500 Robux.

From the underworld . . . to your doorstep

CHICK

Rarity: Common
Availability: Limited
Obtain With: Easter 2020 Egg

The **Chick** was only available at Easter 2020 from a special egg that was given to players for free. This egg had a 100% chance of hatching into a **Chick**. If you didn't get it at the time, the fact it was free means there were plenty around, so you may well be able to trade for one.

It's Easter every day for this Chick.

CHOW-CHOW

Rarity: Legendary
Availability: Permanent
Obtain With: Golden Bone

There are four variants of this pedigree dog in *Adopt Me!*—Black, Tan, Chocolate, and Golden. You need a VIP gamepass so you can access the VIP lounge at the Nursery and buy a **Golden Bone** for 249 Robux.

This pet is a VIP!

CORGI

Rarity: Ultra-Rare
Availability: Permanent
Obtain With: Pet Egg,
Cracked Egg, Royal Egg

The **Corgi** is a type of **dog** known
for being the favorite of Queen
Elizabeth II of England (she had many!).
So if that's your vibe, you'll need a few
of these. Appropriately your best chance
of getting one is from a **Royal Egg**,
and there's a 10% chance.

Grab yourself a posh pooch!

DOG

Rarity: Common
Availability: Permanent
Obtain With: Starter Egg,
Retired Egg

The **Dog** is the other easiest pet in the
game to acquire—though the same
rules apply as with the **Cat**. The **Starter
Egg** has an equal chance of hatching
a **Cat** or a **Dog**, so if you're not a **cat**
person, you'll need to trade with someone
who is or hatch a **Retired Egg**.

Meet your new
best friend.

DONKEY

Rarity: Uncommon
Availability: Permanent
Obtain With: Pet Egg, Cracked Egg, Royal Egg

These small mammals are from the same family as **horses** and are valued working animals—you can ride one, if you're not too heavy! The **Pet Egg** is your best chance of hatching this—just under 12% of **Pet Eggs** hatch a **Donkey**.

You'll get a kick out of this pet!

DUGONG

Rarity: Common
Availability: Limited
Obtain With: Japan Egg

The **Dugong** is a sea mammal and relative of the **manatee**. Real ones are much longer than the version you see in the game, which is rounder and more seal-shaped. It's one of two Common pets to be hatched from the **Japan Egg**.

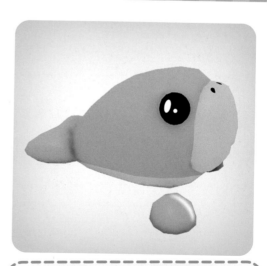

Check out this limited Japan-themed pet.

FENNEC FOX

Rarity: Uncommon
Availability: Permanent
Obtain With: Retired Egg

The **Fennec Fox** is native to the deserts of North Africa, and is known for its very large ears. (The *Adopt Me!* design isn't an exaggeration; they really do have huge ears.) It used to hatch from the three main eggs but can now only be found in the **Retired Egg**.

They're great listeners.

GHOST WOLF

Rarity: Rare
Availability: Limited
Obtain With: Wolf Box

The **Ghost Wolf**, as its name suggests, is a ghostly **wolf** that has no feet and floats above the ground. There's a high chance of obtaining it from a **Wolf Box**—however, seeing as the Halloween Event where the **Wolf Box** was available has ended, you'll have to trade for it or get an unopened **Wolf Box**.

Don't be scared of this spooky Halloween pet.

GINGER CAT

Rarity: Ultra-Rare
Availability: Permanent
Obtain With: Star Rewards

The **Ginger Cat** is the first of six pets players can only obtain from **Star Rewards**. There are lower-value rewards, but this is the cheapest pet. You can claim it once you reach 210 Stars. Note that it isn't just a reskin of the **Cat**—it's slightly larger and rounder.

This pet's just waiting for cat-urday.

GOLDEN LADYBUG

Rarity: Legendary
Availability: Permanent
Obtain With: Diamond Lavender

The **Golden Ladybug** isn't obtained through the **Golden Egg** but by the same method as the **Ladybug**—you must purchase **Diamond Lavender** with Robux and equip it in the Farm Shop. The chance of getting a **Golden Ladybug** via this method is 10%.

Diamonds are a ladybug's best friend.

GOLDEN UNICORN

X

Rarity: Legendary
Availability: Permanent
Obtain With: Star Rewards

. . . .

The final item on the first page of **Star Rewards** for logging in each day (requiring 660 Stars) is the **Golden Egg**, which has an equal chance of hatching into a **Golden Dragon**, a **Golden Griffin**, or a **Golden Unicorn**.

Get your hands on this unique Unicorn!

GUARDIAN LION

X

Rarity: Legendary
Availability: Limited
Obtain With: 500 Robux

. . . .

The **Guardian Lion** is based on traditional Chinese statues that are believed to protect buildings. It was released for the 2021 Lunar New Year event. Unlike the **Lunar Ox**, which was obtained from the **Ox Box**, the **Guardian Lion** only came in one type and had to be purchased with Robux.

Adopt this statue-inspired pet.

HALLOWEEN BLACK MUMMY CAT

Rarity: Uncommon
Availability: Limited
Obtain With: Halloween Mummy Cat Box

The **Halloween Mummy Cat Box** was only available during the Halloween event in 2021. It had a 70% chance of containing a **Halloween Black Mummy Cat**. There were also White and Golden variants, with a 25% and 5% chance.

Happy Halloween!

HALLOWEEN WHITE SKELETON DOG

Rarity: Ultra-rare
Availability: Limited
Obtain With: 1,200 Halloween Candy

Available during the 2021 Halloween event only, this pet could be obtained by earning and then exchanging 1,200 **Halloween Candy**. In the unlikely event of you being able to obtain a Neon version of this pet, you'll see that its entire body glows except for its eyes!

Don't worry, it's perfectly healthy!

IBEX

Rarity: Rare
Availability: Limited
Obtain With: 980 Bucks

. . . .

The **Ibex** is a type of **wild goat**. It was only available in *Adopt Me!* between May 24, 2022 and June 9, 2022. During that time you could purchase it outside the Nursery for 980 Bucks. If you want it now, you'll have to trade for it.

A rare pet with a cool beard

KING PENGUIN

Rarity: Ultra-Rare
Availability: Permanent
Obtain With: Golden Goldfish

. . . .

The **King Penguin** is obtained by buying a **Golden Goldfish** for 225 Robux from the Ice Cream Shop or at the game passes shop. Equip and drop the **Goldfish**, and **Penguins** will gather around. You have the chance of obtaining a **King Penguin** or, rarely, one of its Golden or Diamond variants.

Take a trip to the ice cream shop.

KIRIN

Rarity: Uncommon
Availability: Limited
Obtain With: Mythic Egg

....

The **Kirin** is a creature from East Asian mythology. **Kirin** is the Japanese and Korean name for it, and the *Adopt Me!* version is based on their depiction—like a cross between a **dragon** and a **deer** with a **lion's mane**. It had a 19% chance of hatching from the **Mythic Egg**.

Check out this mythic legend.

KITSUNE

Rarity: Legendary
Availability: Permanent
Obtain With: 600 Robux

....

The **Kitsune** appears in Japanese mythology, in which foxes are believed to be supernatural beings known as **yokai**, that can take on human form. The number of tails a **Kitsune** has shows how wise and powerful it is— this one has an impressive seven! It's available from the Pet Shop.

Seven tails is better than one.

KOI CARP

Rarity: Rare
Availability: Limited
Obtain With: Japan Egg

The **Koi Carp** is a type of **fish** specially bred for ornamental water features—a practice that began in Japan around two hundred years ago. So it's no surprise that it could be obtained from the **Japan Egg**. On the Neon versions, their red scales glow.

Make a splash with this limited pet!

LADYBUG

Rarity: Ultra-Rare
Availability: Permanent
Obtain With: Diamond Lavender

This pet doesn't hatch but is obtained via **Diamond Lavender** from the Farm Shop. Once equipped in your inventory, it starts to attract **Ladybugs** in the shop. One of them will consume the **Diamond Lavender**, at which point it's yours!

Is that lavender?

LUNAR OX

Rarity: Ultra-Rare
Availability: Limited
Obtain With: Ox Box

The Lunar New Year in 2021 brought us the best-named item in all of *Adopt Me!*—the **Ox Box**. Open an **Ox Box**, and you were guaranteed to get an **Ox**. 60% of **Ox Boxes** contained a **normal Ox**, 30% a **Lunar Ox**, and 10% a **Metal Ox**.

Take home your own ox in a box.

LUNAR TIGER

Rarity: Rare
Availability: Limited
Obtain With: Lunar Tiger Box

To coincide with the start of the Lunar Year of the Tiger in February 2022, **Lunar Tiger Boxes** were made available for 350 Bucks. These had a 60% chance of containing a **Lunar Tiger**, a 30% chance of a **Lunar White Tiger**, and a 10% of a **Lunar Gold Tiger**.

You want stripes? This pet's got them!

MOUSE

Rarity: Common
Availability: Permanent
Obtain With: Cracked Egg, Pet Egg

The **Mouse** was introduced as a Common pet in July 2022, when the contents of the **Cracked Egg** were completely overhauled. As one of two Common pets that can hatch from that egg, it became one of the most frequently obtained pets in the game.

Adopt a mouse for your house.

ORANGUTAN

Rarity: Rare
Availability: Permanent
Obtain With: Cracked Egg, Pet Egg, Royal Egg

One of the **great apes** of Southeast Asia, the **Orangutan** has a strong chance of being obtained from the **Royal Egg**. That particular egg has a 37% chance of hatching into a Rare pet, and the **Orangutan** is one of three it can hatch into—meaning a roughly 12% chance.

A great ape, and a greater pet

OTTER

Rarity: Common
Availability: Permanent
Obtain With: Retired Egg

....

Otters are one of a select group of animals (including **foxes** and **tanuki**) to have a special place in Japanese folklore. They're often depicted as shapeshifting tricksters. Though now in the **Retired Egg**, they were very common in *Adopt Me!*, so you can often get them through trading.

You'll never drift apart from this pet.

PARAKEET

Rarity: Rare
Availability: Permanent
Obtain With: Cracked Egg, Pet Egg, Royal Egg

....

The **Parakeet** is a sub-species of **parrot** and comes in several varieties. The one in *Adopt Me!* resembles a **blue Australian budgerigar**. The **Royal Egg** gives you a 12% chance of hatching a **Parakeet**.

Nice to tweet you!

PERSIAN CAT

Rarity: Ultra-Rare
Availability: Limited
Obtain With: Puss in Boots Quest

This **pedigree cat** could only be obtained during a limited event in November 2022 tying in with the film *Puss in Boots: The Last Wish*. Puss in Boots appeared as an NPC in the game and tasked players with finding the components of his outfit, giving the **Persian Cat** as a free reward.

This pet has famous friends.

POODLE

Rarity: Uncommon
Availability: Permanent
Obtain With: Cracked Egg, Pet Egg, Royal Egg

Another type of **dog** obtainable from the three main eggs but easier to get than the **Corgi**, you have the best chance of getting one from a **Pet Egg**—just under 12%. The one in the game resembles a **white miniature poodle**.

One chic puppy

PTERODACTYL

Rarity: Rare
Availability: Limited
Obtain With: Fossil Egg

....

The **Pterodactyl** was one of several **dinosaurs** that was available from the **Fossil Egg** during the Fossil Isle Excavation Event in October 2020. Its coloring is very similar to **Swoop**, a classic *Transformer* from the 1980s, which transformed from a robot into a **pterodactyl**.

Adopt your own dinosaur.

PUMA

Rarity: Uncommon
Availability: Permanent
Obtain With: Retired Egg

....

Also known as the **cougar** or **mountain lion**, the **Puma** is native to North and South America. In real life it has a long, lithe body whereas the *Adopt Me!* version is rounder and cuter. It has slightly less than a 9% chance of hatching from the **Retired Egg**.

This uncommon pet is a great find.

RABBIT

Rarity: Rare
Availability: Permanent
Obtain With: Retired Egg

Confusingly, the original wave of pets obtainable from the three main eggs included a **Bunny** and a **Rabbit**—both of which are white. The **Rabbit** is larger and rounder and has no whiskers. Both can only be obtained from the **Retired Egg** or through trading.

Follow the white rabbit!

RED SQUIRREL

Rarity: Ultra-Rare
Availability: Permanent
Obtain With: 200 Robux

The **Red Squirrel** is one of the more affordable pets that can be bought directly from the Pet Shop, costing just 200 Robux. There's also a Legendary gift, the **Squirrel Car**, which was available in the game for a while.

You'll find it in the Pet Shop tree.

ROBOT

Rarity: Ultra-Rare
Availability: Permanent
Obtain With: Cracked Egg,
Pet Egg, Royal Egg

This is the second robot to be introduced into *Adopt Me!* (after the **Robo Dog**, a limited pet that could be bought for 600 Robux). Your best chance of obtaining it is via the **Royal Egg**, which offers a 10% chance of hatching into a **Robot**.

Take home a pet of the future!

ROYAL PALACE SPANIEL

Rarity: Ultra-Rare
Availability: Permanent
Obtain With: 299 Robux

There are lots of **spaniel** breeds, but the **Royal Palace Spaniel** isn't one of them. The spaniel with the closest royal association is the **King Charles spaniel**, but this one more resembles a **springer spaniel**. It's available to buy from the Pet Shop.

Adopt one's own Royal Spaniel.

SADO MOLE

Rarity: Common
Availability: Limited
Obtain With: Japan Egg

. . . .

The **Sado Mole**, also known as **Toduka's mole**, is a type of **mole** that only lives on Sado Island, just off the northwestern coast of Japan. It was one of the two most commonly obtained pets from the **Japan Egg**, with an 11% chance.

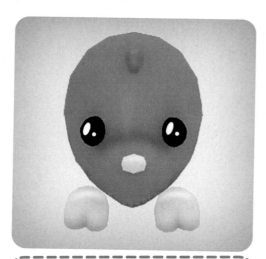

This pet was common for a limited time.

SASQUATCH

Rarity: Ultra-Rare
Availability: Limited
Obtain With: Woodland Egg

. . . .

The **Sasquatch** is also popularly known as **Bigfoot**. There have been many, many reported sightings of this mythical ape-like creature in the forests of North America, but no proof of its existence has ever been found. It had a 17% chance of hatching from the **Mythic Egg**.

Mystery solved!

SHIBA INU

Rarity: Ultra-Rare
Availability: Permanent
Obtain With: Retired Egg

The **Shiba Inu** is a small Japanese breed of **hunting dog**, known for its high-pitched scream. *Adopt Me!* includes a version of the red breed—the rarest of the three **dogs** that hatch from the **Retired Egg**, with a 7.5% chance of being obtained.

This pet only hunts fun times.

SLOTH

Rarity: Ultra-Rare
Availability: Permanent
Obtain With: 199 Robux

The **Sloth** is the cheapest pet that can be bought from the Pet Shop. At 199 Robux it is one Robux (Robuck?) cheaper than the **Red Squirrel**. Not to be confused with the **Ground Sloth**, a limited pet hatched from **Fossil Eggs**.

A great pet to hang out with

SNOW CAT

Rarity: Uncommon
Availability: Permanent
Obtain With: Retired Egg

The **Snow Cat** isn't an actual breed of **cat**. It's one of two **cats** available from the **Retired Egg**, and though it's Uncommon, it's actually more likely to be obtained than the **Common Cat**. It has a chance of just under 9% compared to the **Cat's** 5%.

Adopt your own cold kitten.

SNOW PUMA

Rarity: Rare
Availability: Permanent
Obtain With: Retired Egg

In the real world, pure **white pumas** are incredibly rare (one has been spotted in Brazil). However, in *Adopt Me!* such creatures are merely Rare and can be obtained from the **Retired Egg** with a chance of just under 7%.

Will you find this paw-some pet?

SPIDER CRAB

Rarity: Ultra-Rare
Availability: Limited
Obtain With: Japan Egg

There are lots of species of **Spider Crab**, but the one in *Adopt Me!* is based on the largest of all, the **Japanese Spider Crab**. (The legs of a real one are pointed, rather than ending in little circular feet.) There was a 6.66% chance of getting one from a **Japan Egg**.

Good thing pets don't need shoes!

STINGRAY

Rarity: Common
Availability: Limited
Obtain With: Ocean Egg

The **Stingray** family covers a wide range of **fish**, and this one is based on an **eagle ray**, identifiable by the pointed tips of its fins. It was the most commonly hatched pet from the **Ocean Egg**. You can't put shoes on it because it doesn't have feet!

Some pets live underwater in the real world.

SWORDFISH

Rarity: Ultra-Rare
Availability: Permanent
Obtain With: Cracked Egg, Pet Egg, Royal Egg

The **Swordfish** is a very common type of **fish**, found in temperate and tropical seas all around the world. However, it's Ultra-Rare in *Adopt Me!* and is most likely to hatch from a **Royal Egg**, with a 10% chance.

Don't worry, it's not sharp!

TANUKI

Rarity: Uncommon
Availability: Limited
Obtain With: Japan Egg

The **Tanuki** is a **raccoon-like** animal native to Japan, and it has a special status in Japanese folklore. **Tanuki yokai** (supernatural beings) are featured in many traditional stories, often depicted as mischievous shapeshifters. So it's no surprise this pet was limited to the **Japan Egg**.

Adopt your own cute Japanese critter.

TASMANIAN TIGER

Rarity: Common
Availability: Limited
Obtain With: Fossil Egg

Sadly the **Tasmanian Tiger** (or **thylacine**) no longer exists in the wild, having been hunted to extinction by humans in the 1930s after **dingoes** took over many of its habitats. It's the most recently-extinct animal to be included in the **Fossil Egg**.

Check out this incredible extinct pet.

THERAPY DOG

Rarity: Uncommon
Availability: Limited
Obtain With: Task from Patty

The **Therapy Dog** was available for a short time, starting in late 2022. It could be obtained for free by finding the NPC **Patty** by the Playground and then carrying out the task she gave you and healing a pet or baby three times.

This pet was sponsored by the Great Ormond Street Hospital.

TOUCAN

Rarity: Ultra-Rare
Availability: Permanent
Obtain With: Star Rewards

The **Toucan** is the second of four pets that can be obtained from the first page of the **Star Rewards**. Maintain a streak of playing every day and collect 400 Stars to unlock the **Toucan**, which is based on the appearance of the **toco toucan**, the most common type.

Adopt this toucan—it's a star!

WOLPERTINGER

Rarity: Common
Availability: Limited
Obtain With: Mythic Egg

What's a **Wolpertinger**? Well, it's a creature from German folklore, a cross between a **hare**, a **deer**, and a **duck** that supposedly lives in the forests. The version in *Adopt Me!* has fangs that make it look like a **vampire**, too.

Three animals—but one mythical pet

WOOLLY MAMMOTH

Rarity: Rare
Availability: Limited
Obtain With: Fossil Egg

The **Woolly Mammoth** emerged about 800,000 years ago and images of it can be found in prehistoric cave paintings. It's another of the extinct animals featured in the **Fossil Egg** and is similar in construction to the **Elephant**, with added tusks and shaggy fur.

Adopt your own fossilized friend.

YELLOW BUTTERFLY

Rarity: Rare
Availability: Limited
Obtain With: Leaf

In August 2022 a new building was added—the **Butterfly Sanctuary**. There, a **Leaf** could be bought for 899 Bucks or a **Golden Leaf** for 199 Bucks, which could be used to tame different colors of **Butterfly**. The **Butterfly Sanctuary** was removed from the game after two weeks.

Take this pet home to your own sanctuary.

ZEBRA

Rarity: Rare
Availability: Permanent
Obtain With: Cracked Egg,
Pet Egg, Royal Egg

The **Zebra** is a Rare pet, which is the most likely type to be obtained from a **Royal Egg**. It's also, in our opinion, the best-looking of all the Neon variants because (as you might have guessed!) its glow comes from its stripes.

A great pet to
earn your stripes

ZODIAC MINION CHICK

Rarity: Legendary
Availability: Limited
Obtain With: Zodiac Minion Egg

The **Zodiac Minion Chick** was put into the game as part of a tie-in with the movie *Minions: The Rise of Gru*. The egg could be obtained for free and guaranteed a **Zodiac Minion Chick**, making this the first wholly free Legendary pet.

A gift from Gru

WHAT IS YOUR IDEAL PET?

You're bound to have favorite pets in *Adopt Me!*—but which one truly suits your personality? Take our quiz and find out!

What do you like to wear for a fun day out?
A) Your most stylish outfit
B) Sports gear and running shoes
C) A swimsuit and goggles
D) A vampire outfit
E) A magical cloak that makes the wearer invisible

What's the best kind of gift you can receive?
A) Gift certificates. Or just cash!
B) Travel and experiences are better than things.
C) Bubble bath
D) A huge bucket of candy
E) Books—the more imaginative the better!

Apart from *Adopt Me!*, what's your favorite *Roblox* game?
A) *Meep City*
B) *Super Striker League*
C) *Scuba Diving at Quill Lake*
D) *Piggy*
E) *Dungeon Quest*

What's your favorite kind of music?
A) Pure pop
B) Dance music with a fast beat
C) Whalesong
D) Horror movie soundtracks
E) Epic heroic theme songs

....

Where would you most like to live?
A) In a modern city apartment
B) Somewhere with plenty of open space
C) On the beach
D) In a haunted house
E) On a space station

....

Choose your favorite film from this list . . .
A) *Frozen*
B) *Space Jam: A New Legacy*
C) *Avatar: The Way of Water*
D) *The Nightmare Before Christmas*
E) *Guardians of the Galaxy*

Turn over the page for your result . . .

ANSWERS

MOSTLY A's – ROYAL PALACE SPANIEL

You're a socially plugged-in person, and you need a dog that's both pedigree and expensive!

MOSTLY B's – PUMA

You're an active person who loves sports and being outdoors, and you need a pet who can keep up with you. The **Puma** is perfect!

MOSTLY C's – STINGRAY

You love to be on the beach and in the ocean, so what you need is a pet you can go swimming with, like the **Stingray**.

MOSTLY D's – CERBERUS

You like spookiness and jumpscares, and any Halloween pet would be great for you—but we chose **Cerberus** because he's available from the Pet Shop.

MOSTLY E's – KITSUNE

You like to live in a world of imagination, so instead of a regular old pet from the real world, how about a mystical seven-tailed fox from Japanese mythology?